Help Me Understand

What Happens When I Go to the Hospital?

Dwayne Hicks

PowerKiDS press.

NEW YORK

Published in 2019 by The Rosen Publishing Group, Inc.
29 East 21st Street, New York, NY 10010

First Edition

Editor: Greg Roza
Book Design: Rachel Rising

Photo Credits: Cover, Pressmaster/Shutterstock.com; p. 4 Spiroview Inc/Shutterstock.com; pp. 5, 9, 13 Monkey Business Images/Shutterstock.com; p. 6 Catalin Rusnac/Shutterstock.com; p. 7 Jeff Whyte/Shutterstock.com; p. 8 (hand, head, chest) itsmejust/Shutterstock.com; pp. 11, 21 Tungphoto/Shutterstock.com; p. 12 Ruslan Guzov/Shutterstock.com; p. 14 Antonio Guillem/Shutterstock.com; p. 15 1981 Rustic Studio kan/Shutterstock.com; p. 17 wavebreakmedia/Shutterstock.com; p. 19 Bangkoker/Shutterstock.com; p. 20 LarsZ/Shutterstock.com; p. 22 kurhan/Shutterstock.com.

Library of Congress Cataloging-in-Publication Data

Names: Hicks, Dwayne, author.
Title: What happens when I go to the hospital? / Dwayne Hicks.
Description: New York : PowerKids Press, [2019] | Series: Help me understand
   | Includes index.
Identifiers: LCCN 2018028657| ISBN 9781538348062 (library bound) | ISBN
   9781538348055 (pbk.) | ISBN 9781538348161 (6 pack)
Subjects: LCSH: Hospitals–Juvenile literature. | Medical care–Juvenile
   literature. | Medical personnel–Juvenile literature.
Classification: LCC RA963.5 .H53 2019 | DDC 362.11–dc23
LC record available at https://lccn.loc.gov/2018028657

Manufactured in the United States of America

CPSIA Compliance Information: Batch #CWPK19. For Further Information contact Rosen Publishing, New York, New York at 1-800-237-9932

Contents

Something New and Scary

Have you ever gone to a hospital before? Maybe you've visited a family member who was staying in a hospital. Or maybe you went to visit the doctor. A hospital is a place where people get **medical** care. Unlike a doctor's office, a hospital is usually big and there are many people there.

It can be scary when you have to go to the hospital, but sometimes it helps to know more about it. You can be prepared!

Hospital workers come from many different backgrounds. They're all there to help!

Inside the Walls

Usually, people go to the hospital for **emergencies** or for bigger medical problems. Some people go to have **surgery**. Some people go to take different kinds of medical tests.

Hospitals have different areas for different reasons. These areas are called departments. Most have a department just for kids like you. If you have to make plans to stay at the hospital for something, you might be able to visit and see what it's like first.

Sometimes hospitals are just for children. They still have many different departments.

Children's Hospital

EMERGENCY →

EMERGENCY →   EMERGENCY →

There to Help

Hospitals are filled with workers who are trained to help you. Many different kinds of doctors specialize in many different parts of the body. Nurses help doctors take care of you.

Many other hospital workers are there to help, too. Some people take **X-rays** and do other tests. Some workers bring you food. There will be people who can talk to you if you're scared or worried. You will see many other **patients** as well.

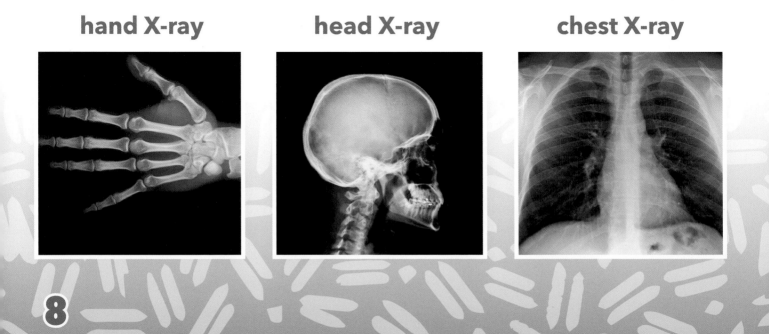

hand X-ray   head X-ray   chest X-ray

A doctor who works with kids is called a pediatrician.

Packing and Planning

If you're going to the hospital for a planned surgery, such as having your **tonsils** taken out, you'll be able to plan before you get there. You might be able to visit the children's area.

You can talk to your doctor about what it will be like during and after your surgery. You can pack a bag yourself and take along a stuffed animal, games, or some books to read while you stay there.

You might be able to wear your own pajamas or clothes in the hospital, but you often have to wear a special hospital robe.

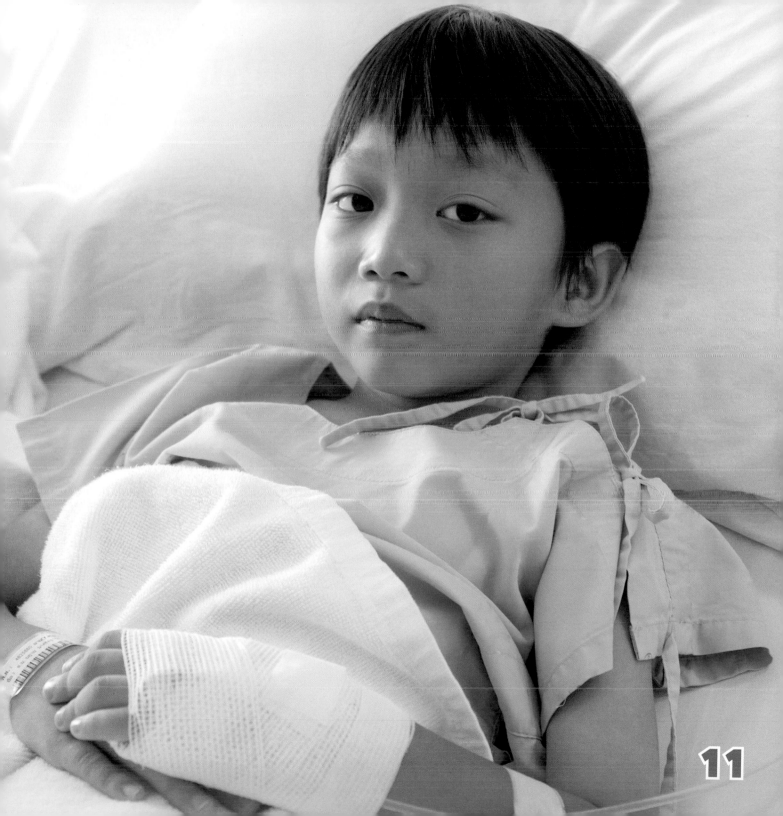

11

So Many Questions

When you're at the hospital, your parents will probably have to fill out many forms and pieces of paper that tell the hospital about you and your medical problem. You might have to answer a lot of questions, too.

If you don't understand a question, ask your parents, a nurse, or another adult for help. The more they know about you, the better they can take care of you. You can ask questions, too.

If you're worried, asking questions can help.

If You Have an Operation

If you have to have surgery, you'll likely meet someone whose job it is to make sure you sleep during the **operation**. This person is called an anesthesiologist.

When it's time for surgery, you'll ride on a bed on wheels to the operating room, which is where doctors do operations. Afterward, you'll wake up in a special room where nurses will be able to check on you until you can go back to your own room.

surgeon →

You might not be able to eat before your surgery so the medicine can work properly.

Recovery

You might be in pain after your surgery. If you are, it's important to tell a doctor or a nurse. They will do their best to give you medicines to help you feel better.

Resting after surgery is very important, too. You might have your own hospital room, but you might have to share it with another child. If you share, remember that your roommate is **recovering**, too. Even if you're feeling better, they may need rest.

You might have to ride in a wheelchair to get around for a while instead of walking. This is to make sure you don't fall.

→

It's an Emergency

Sometimes visits to the hospital aren't planned. These visits are called emergencies. If you fall and break your leg or if you get sick suddenly, your doctor might have your parents take you to the emergency room, or ER.

The ER is a place in the hospital for people who need care quickly. You also might have to ride in an **ambulance** to the hospital. Don't be scared! This is a way to get you there quickly and safely.

You might have to wait at the emergency room. People with the biggest emergencies go first. ⟶

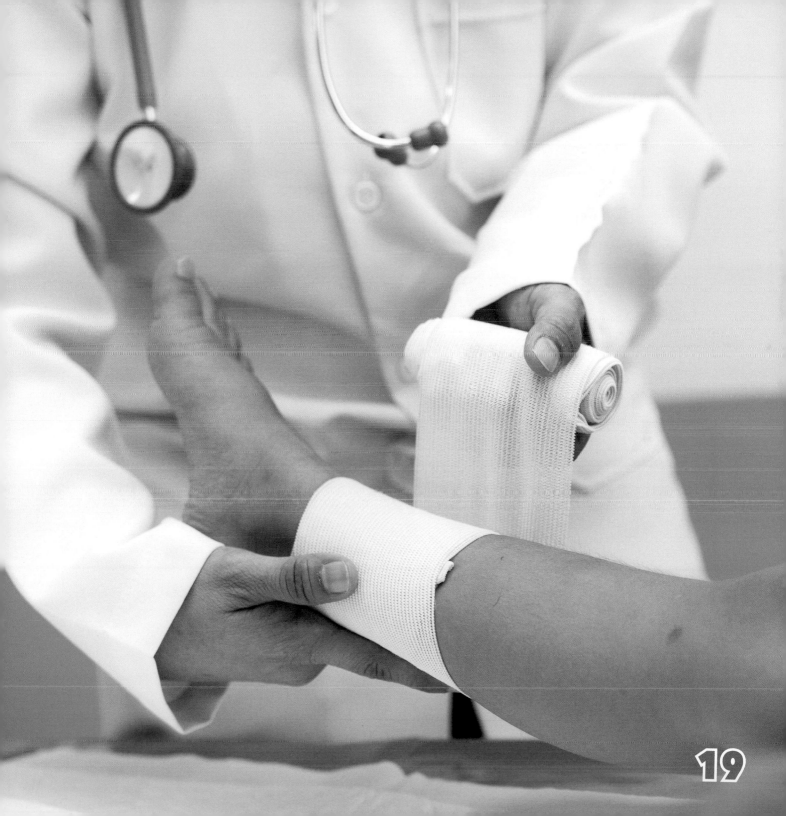

19

If you have to go to the emergency room, the doctors and nurses might be able to help you and then send you home. However, they might keep you in the hospital longer if you need more help and care. Sometimes this is so the doctors and nurses can keep an eye on you to make sure you're getting better. Sometimes, you might need surgery or special medicines. It may seem scary, but it's to help you get better.

In the hospital, you'll be able to call for help quickly if you have a problem. You just have to push a button to get help.

 CALL

CANCEL

Helping Hands

You might just have to stay at the hospital a few hours for an emergency. Or you might have to stay longer if you need surgery or are very sick. This can be scary.

It's important to tell people how you're feeling, whether you're in pain or if you're worried or scared. Many hospitals have **counselors** and religious leaders who can talk to you about what you're going through. Hospital workers are there to help!

Glossary

ambulance: A car or van used for taking sick or hurt people to the hospital.

counselor: Someone who counsels, or listens and gives people help.

emergency: Something unexpected that needs quick action.

medical: Having to do with care given by doctors.

operation: When a doctor cuts into someone's body to fix or remove something.

patient: Someone receiving medical care.

recover: To become healthy again after being hurt or sick.

surgery: A medical treatment that involves operations.

tonsil: One of two soft parts on the inside of your throat.

X-ray: A picture of the inside of the body.

Index

Websites

Due to the changing nature of Internet links, PowerKids Press has developed an online list of websites related to the subject of this book. This site is updated regularly. Please use this link to access the list: www.powerkidslinks.com/hmu/hospital